Our names are Bonnie and Ronnie. We're like most brothers and sisters, except that we're twins. If you're a twin like us, there's one question you are asked all the time: "What's it like being a twin?" In this book, we'll try to answer this question once and for all. In the process, we'll look at how twins are created, we'll talk about lots of famous and amazing twins—including animal twins—we'll give you some survival tips, and we'll show you how to have fun, twin-style!

Nicole Rubel

Twice As Nice
What It's Like to Be a Twin

Farrar, Straus and Giroux

New York

For my twin sister, Bonnie, who has always *been*, and will always *be*, in my pictures

www.fsgkidsbooks.com

Library of Congress Cataloging-in-Publication Data
Rubel, Nicole.
    Twice as nice : what it's like to be a twin / Nicole Rubel.— 1st ed.
        p.   cm.
    Summary: Presents facts, anecdotes, studies, opinions, and advice on the topic of twins.
    ISBN 0-374-31836-0
    1. Twins—Juvenile literature.   2. Multiple birth—Juvenile literature.   [1. Twins.]   I. Title.

HQ777.35.R83 2005
306.875—dc22

                                                                        2003054168

Contents

We Love Being Twins!

We're never alone.

Everyone makes a fuss.

We share everything.

Being a Twin Stinks!

We share everything.

Bonnie, can I climb up?

Twins! Oh, you two are so cute. I could eat you up. You're so lucky. You have each other forever. I always wanted to be a twin . . .

We're never alone.

Everyone makes a fuss.

Where Do Twins Come From?

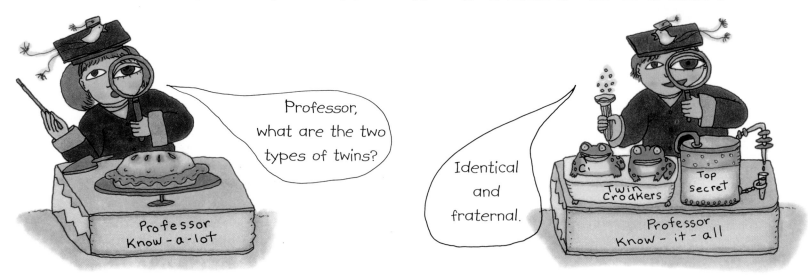

Identical twins are like two halves of the same pie.
One fertilized egg inside a mother divides into two sections, resulting in identical babies.

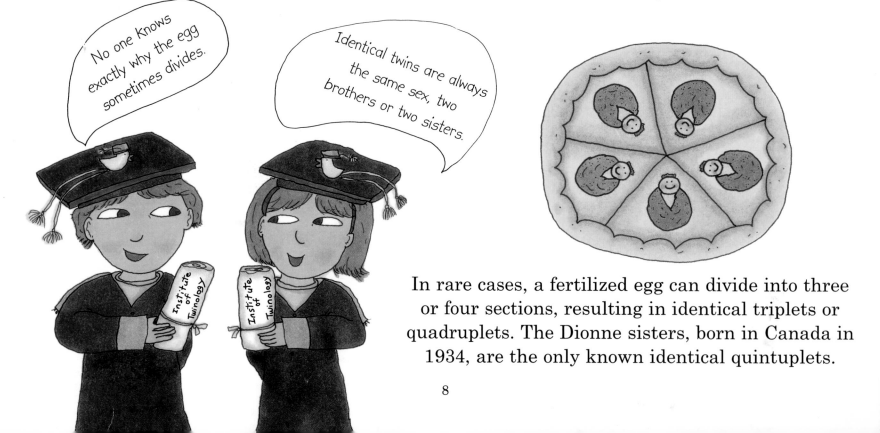

In rare cases, a fertilized egg can divide into three or four sections, resulting in identical triplets or quadruplets. The Dionne sisters, born in Canada in 1934, are the only known identical quintuplets.

Fraternal twins are like two separate whole pies.
Two different fertilized eggs inside a mother grow into two different babies
at exactly the same time.

Fraternal twins can be
a brother and sister, two
brothers . . .

. . . or two sisters, like us!
Most twins are fraternal.

If a woman is a fraternal twin herself, she is more likely than a
non-twin to give birth to fraternal twins.

The Jim Twins

While identical twins look the same, they are never completely alike. They have their own personalities, and exhibit differences in many ways. But they can have a lot of amazing things in common, like the famous "Jim Twins." In 1979, newspapers around the country publicized the meeting of identical twins Jim Springer and Jim Lewis, who had been raised separately. When they met at age thirty-nine, Jim and Jim (both six feet tall and 180 pounds) discovered:

Each twin had owned a dog named Toy. Both enjoyed stock-car racing and disliked baseball.

Each twin vacationed with his family on the same Florida beach. Jim and Jim had each been married

twice. Their first wives were both named Linda; their second, Betty. Each had a son with the same name:

James Alan and James Allan. Both bit their fingernails, and both suffered from migraine headaches.

Both scattered love letters to their wives around the house.

What Are the Odds?

Today, out of every thousand babies born . . .

. . . thirty of them will be twins!

In the United States, there is one set of twins born for every sixty-six births.

Out of every thirty twins born in the United States, about twenty will be fraternal and ten will be identical.

Of the roughly four million babies born in the United States this year, 120,000 will be twins, 6,500 will be triplets, and 500 will be quadruplets.

WAHH!!!

What's the trouble here? We received a lot of calls at headquarters!

Twins around the World

Some ancient cultures believed that the birth of twins was a good omen that foretold a season of plentiful hunting and fishing. Other cultures believed that twins had special powers over the weather.

A steady diet of twins can be had at Twins restaurant in New York City, which employs twin waiters and waitresses.

In other ancient cultures, twins were thought to bring bad luck. Some cultures believed that twin babies were fathered by different men or by evil spirits.

In Scandinavian myths, there are many stories about the gods Balder and his blind twin brother, Hoder, by whom he was killed after they fought over a goddess.

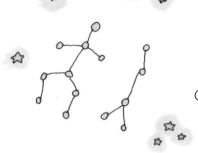

In the night sky sits the Gemini constellation, representing Castor and Pollux, twin warriors in Greek mythology. "Gemini" is Latin for "the twins."

In Africa, twinning occurs more frequently than anywhere else.

Twins Days Festival   Saturday 8-3-02

Nearly three thousand sets of twins gather once a year for the Twins Days Festival in Twinsburg, Ohio.

In eighteenth-century Russia, a Mrs. Fyodor Vassilyev gave birth to sixteen pairs of twins in addition to seven sets of triplets and four sets of quadruplets. She had a total of sixty-nine children.

The Yoruba people in Nigeria are the world champions for giving birth to twins. Something in their diet of locally grown yams may be the cause. One out of eleven Yorubas is a twin.

Animal Twins

Like humans, some animals such as gorillas, elephants, and sea otters usually produce only one offspring at a time. Often these are animals whose babies are large in size and require a lot of work to feed and protect. For them, twins are rare.

Here are Chinta and Towan, orangutan twins at eleven weeks, at the Woodland Park Zoo in Seattle, Washington.

Amiri and Ayana, twin lowland gorillas, live at the Oklahoma City Zoo.

Among some animals, twins are not uncommon. These include lemurs, moose, pronghorn antelope, mountain goats, polar bears, giant pandas, and domesticated sheep and goats. A few unusual animals such as tamarins, marmosets, and New Zealand geckos give birth to twins almost always. The nine-banded armadillo nearly always gives birth to identical quadruplets!

Rather than focus their energy on raising just a few babies safely, many animals produce tens, hundreds, or even thousands of tiny offspring, "hoping" that some will survive the threat of predators, competition, and harsh environments.

Who Is Smarter? (and Other Dumb Twin Questions)

What's it like being a twin?

Who was born first?

Ask the stork who brought us.

I don't know.
What's it like not being a twin?

Why aren't you dressed
alike, like real twins?

Wow, am I seeing double?

Yes, maybe you should get your eyes checked.

Real twins robbed us
earlier and left us these shorts.

If I pinch your arm, will your twin feel it?
No, but you will!
Do you two have the same dreams?
Yes, we dream about meeting people who don't ask silly questions.
DUNCE
Do you often trade places and fool people?
Yes, you're not really talking to me; you're talking to my twin.
Can your mother tell you apart?
Our mom's not dumb, but you are.

The Story of Jacob and Esau

According to the Bible, Rebecca, wife of Isaac, gave birth to twin boys. The two babies wrestled in Rebecca's womb over who was to be born first. Esau won. He was red and hairy. Jacob came second. He was pink and hairless.

Even though the boys were twins, they were very different. Jacob liked to stay at home and help his mother. Esau loved to run outside and hunt animals, which pleased his father. Since Esau was the firstborn, he was Isaac's heir and would become head of the household when his father died. This made Jacob jealous.

One day Esau came home from his hunt empty-handed. He smelled Jacob's delicious bean soup. "I'm dying of hunger," he said. "How about some soup?" Jacob wanted to be the head of the household when he grew up, so he said, "Will you trade your birthright for a bowl of bean soup?" Esau agreed. Jacob made Esau swear to God first, and he did. Then Jacob gave him a nice big bowl of soup.

18

Many years later, Isaac was blind and dying.
He asked Esau to go hunting and bring him fresh meat.
While he was gone, Rebecca, who favored her second-born, suggested that Jacob kill two goats and she would cook the meat for Isaac.

Rebecca dressed Jacob
in Esau's clothes and put the
goatskins on his neck and
hands to make him hairy.
Isaac touched Jacob's hairy
hands and wondered why he
heard the voice of Jacob
but felt the hands of Esau.
Still, Isaac blessed his son
and ate the meat.

Later, Esau returned with his meat. He cooked it
and served it to Isaac. Isaac was confused and upset.
"I've already blessed whoever brought me meat before."
"Bless me, too, Father," Esau asked.
"I'm sorry, Esau, my firstborn son," said Isaac. "Your brother, Jacob, has tricked you. For now, you will have to serve him, but one day you will grow restless and break free from his control."

19

Amazing Twins!

Circus performers Elsie and Serenity Smith
call themselves Gemini Trapeze and teach workshops in aerial
acrobatics all around the United States.

Since their first television audition in 1987
at age seven months, fraternal twins Mary-Kate and Ashley
Olsen have gone on to star in television shows and movies and
launch their own brand of books, clothing, and teen accessories.

In the superstar pop-music trio known as the Bee Gees,
twins Robin and Maurice Gibb sang with older brother Barry.
Together they earned seven Grammy Awards.

Veena and Neena, also known as the Bellytwins,
are belly-dancing identical twins in California who sometimes
perform with pythons and boa constrictors.

In 1914, twin cowgirls Ethyl and Juanita Parry saddled up with the Miller Brothers' 101 Ranch Wild West Show near Ponca City, Oklahoma.

Chang and Eng, the "original" Siamese Twins, were born in Siam in 1811 joined at the chest. For years, they made a living as a famous circus act in Europe and America. They settled in North Carolina and were successful farmers; in 1844, they adopted "Bunker" as their last name and became American citizens.

Twin brothers Claude and Cliff Trenier and their family band had a hit "swinging blues" song in 1951.

In the 1940s, singing twins Lee and Lyn Wilde were promised the lead roles in a pair of Hollywood movies about twins, but a new editing technique enabled a famous star to play both parts in each film.

More Amazing Twins!

Twins Reggie and Ronnie Kray were two of Britain's most notorious gangsters. They spent the last three decades of their lives behind bars.

Born in Russia, Raphael and Moses Soyer were both famous artists in New York City. They each liked to paint and draw people. In 1962, Raphael painted this portrait of himself and his twin.

Weighing over 750 pounds each, Billy and Benny McGuire were the world's heaviest twins. Shortly after this cross-country promotional ride for a motorcycle company, they started their successful career in professional wrestling.

As Abigail Van Buren and Ann Landers,
identical twin sisters Pauline Esther Friedman and Esther
Pauline Friedman from Iowa wrote competing advice columns
that each ran in hundreds of newspapers around the world.

According to legend, abandoned twin princes
Romulus and Remus grew up to found the city of Rome on the
banks of the river where they had been tended by a she-wolf
until rescued by a royal shepherd.

Identical twin sisters June and Jennifer Gibbons in England
had such a hard time communicating with others that they
made a pact to speak only to each other. Their sad story is
told in a book and a movie called The Silent Twins.

Since 1904, millions of readers have followed the
adventures of the Bobbsey Twins—Bert and Nan, Freddie
and Flossie—in what is probably the longest-running
children's book series of all time.

Twin Riddles

Which streets do twins prefer to travel?

Two-way.

What is a twin sister crossed with a lot of wind?

A twister.

What were the twin hens laughing at?

Double yokes.

What kind of stars do twins like?

Ones that twin-kle.

What did the slobbering warthog say to his twin?
You're my spitting image.

Which kinds of parents have twins?
Tired ones.

Tra la la!

What kind of music do twins like best?
Duets.

What do you do if twin tigers are walking toward you?
Run twice as fast!

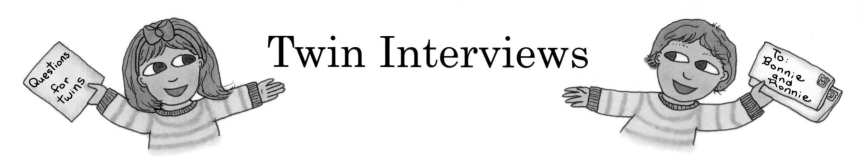

Twin Interviews

Matt and Ryan England (age 7)

Do you enjoy sharing birthdays?
Ryan: I don't really like it. I wish I had my own day.

Do you enjoy sharing clothes?
Matt: No, because we have to share and we start arguing. Ryan wants to wear what I want to wear. He's into fighting, and he's stronger and can give me a fat lip. I used to be strong, but he started practicing and got better.

Adrian and Arcelia Arteaga–Del Toro (age 6)

Do you know what your brother's going to say a lot of the time?
Arcelia: Yes, sometimes I guess what he's going to say or choose, like cake or a game. Sometimes when I'm sleeping I think about what he'll pick, and when I wake up I'm right!

How do you feel when your friends confuse you with your twin?
Adrian: They don't, she's a girl!

26

Megan and Erin Kibby (age 8)

Do you often dress alike?
Megan: No, only when we have to.
Erin: No, people get mixed up, and I'm sick and tired of being called Megan.

How do you feel when your friends confuse you with your twin?
Erin: Friends? I don't care, but they do it every day. If they did it once a week, it'd be better.

Allie and Katie Nunemaker (age 7)

Do you enjoy sharing birthdays?
Allie: Sometimes. This year I want to have my own birthday.
Katie: Yes, this year I want my own birthday.

How will you do that since your birthday is on the same day?
Allie: I will have my birthday in the morning, no, in the night.
Katie: No, I want the night.

Survival Secrets for Twins

Your parents or friends will never know you the way your twin does.
Cherish the unique twin bond you have.

Cut loose from your twin and find your own
activities and hobbies. You can always share them later.

Some twins find it scary to be alone. Try spending time without your twin for short periods, then longer ones. You'll both be stronger and learn who you are apart from each other.

Try not to be jealous when your twin makes new friends. Remember, no one can replace you. And think of the many new friends you can have if you share.

Advice for Parents, Teachers, and Friends of Twins

Please remember to take photos of us separately.

We have names. Please don't call us "the twins" or "twinnies."

Please try to tell us apart. If you're still confused, ask us to wear different watches, necklaces, or baseball caps.

Why do we have to wear matching sailor suits to Grandma's?

Look, even the dog's going to match us!

Let us decide if we want to dress alike. Some twins enjoy it and some don't.

31

Notes and Acknowledgments

Special thanks to Dr. Nancy L. Segal, author of *Entwined Lives: Twins and What They Tell Us about Human Behavior* (New York: Plume, 2000), for her help and support. **Page 9:** Photograph of Allie and Katie Nunemaker courtesy of Jan and Gerald Nunemaker. **Page 10:** For the full story on the Jim Twins' amazing reunion, see "Reunion of Identical Twins, Raised Apart, Reveals Some Astonishing Similarities" by Donald Dale Jackson in *Smithsonian Magazine*, October 1980. **Page 11:** My statistics are drawn from several sources, including U.S. birth numbers for 2001 from the National Center for Health Statistics, *www.cdc.gov/nchs*, as well as *www.twinsmagazine.com/factsstats .html* and *mypage.direct.ca/c/csamson/multiples/twinbasics2.html*. **Pages 12–13:** For information on twin myths, see "How the World Views Twins" by Alice M. Vollmar in *The Twinship Sourcebook: Your Guide to Understanding Multiples,* compiled by the editors of *Twins* magazine (Englewood, Colo.: Twins Magazine, 1997); "Twins in Myth, Folklore, and Literature" in *Twins and Supertwins* by Amram Scheinfeld (Baltimore: Penguin, 1973); "Twin Myths" in *Raising Twins from Birth through Adolescence* by Eileen M. Pearlman and Jill Alison Gannon (New York: Harper, 2000); and "The Fascination with Multiple Births" in *Having Twins and More* by Elizabeth Noble with Leo Sorger (Boston: Houghton Mifflin, 2003). Twins restaurant photograph courtesy of Debbie and Lisa Ganz, *www.twinsworld.com*. Twins Days photograph courtesy of Twins Days Festival Committee, Inc., Twinsburg, Ohio; for more informa-tion, *www.twinsdays.org*. Photograph of African twins (from Rwanda) courtesy of Mekael Volimte, *www.innergardenart.com/twinsS.html*. Fyodor Vassilyev's wife's incredible productivity is mentioned in many sources, including the National Organization of Mothers of Twins Clubs Web site, *www.nomotc.org*, although Lawrence Wright gives significantly different name spellings and dates in *Twins and What They Tell Us about Who We Are* (New York: John Wiley & Sons, 1997), p. 100. For information on the yam diet influencing the twinning rate among Yoruba women, see "The Material Culture of Twins in West Africa" by Rachel Ndi, posted at the Simon Fraser University Museum of Archaeology and Ethnology Web site, *www.sfu.ca/archaeology/museum/ndi/ mystudy.html*, and "Twins Poser for Fertility Boffs" by Ade Obisesan at the Science in Africa Web site, *www.scienceinafrica.co.za/twins.htm*. **Pages 14–15:** I consulted many sources to verify typical litter sizes for animals in text and art, especially *Walker's Mammals of the World* Online, *www.press.jhu.edu/ books/walker/toc.html*. Thanks to Dana Payne, Collection Manager at the Woodland Park Zoo, for information on animal twins and the photograph of orangutan twins. Photograph of the twin lowland gorillas courtesy of Joe Smith of the Oklahoma City Zoo. **Pages 20–21:** Gemini Trapeze photograph courtesy of Elsie and Serenity Smith, *www.trapezetwins.com*. Information about the Olsen twins from the Mary-Kate and Ashley Official Timeline, *www.mary-kateandashley.com*. Information on the Brothers Gibb from *www.beegeesonline.com*. Photograph of Veena and Neena courtesy of the Bellytwins, *www.veenaandneena.com*. Thanks to Al Stehno for his help with information on the Parry sisters; their photograph is reproduced from *Cowgirls* by Judy Crandall (Atglen, Pa.: Schiffer Publications, 1994). Trenier Brothers photograph courtesy of Slick Trenier on behalf of the Treniers; for discography of the Treniers, see *www.rockabilly.net/milttrenier/bio.shtml*. For concise biographies of Chang and Eng Bunker, see *www.barnum-museum.org/orig/ html/chang.html*. The Wilde Twins photograph courtesy of Lee Wilde Cathcart; the movies were MGM's *A Stolen Life* and *The Dark Mirror*, both made in 1946, which starred Bette Davis and Olivia de Havilland, respectively. **Pages 22–23:** *Double Portrait*, c. 1962, by Raphael Soyer; © Estate of Raphael Soyer, private collection, courtesy of the Forum Gallery, New York. For a string of articles on the Kray brothers, search on Reggie Kray at the BBC News Web site, *http://news.bbc.co.uk*. The McGuire twins' story is detailed in Greg Oliver's obituary for SLAM! Wrestling, *www.stampeders.com/SlamWrestling BiosM/mcguire-can.html*; their photograph courtesy of Scott Teal, *www.1wrestlinglegends.com*. Photograph of Abigail Van Buren and Ann Landers courtesy of AP/Wide World. Marjorie Wallace details the story of the Gibbons sisters in *The Silent Twins* (New York: Prentice Hall, 1986); for recent developments, see Hilton Als's "We Two Made One" in *The New Yorker*, December 4, 2000. James D. Keeline has posted his authoritative history of the Bobbsey Twins series at *www.keeline.com/StratemeyerSyndicate.html*. **Pages 26–27:** Thanks to Sharron McElmeel and Kathy Hartman for arranging my twin interviews. Thanks to the twins and their families for supplying photographs and answering my questions. **Pages 28–31:** Some of my advice for twins and non-twins is adapted from *Dancing Naked in Front of the Fridge and Other Lessons from Twins* (Vancouver, B.C.: Fair Winds, 1999); thanks to authors Nancy J. Sipes and Janna S. Sipes. Photograph of Victorian twins with hats courtesy of the Florida State Archives.

Well, that's it from us! We hope we've helped you see that in a lot of ways being a twin really can be twice as nice. And the next time somebody asks, "What's it like being a twin?" here's a great answer (which happens to be true): "Being a twin is like having a best friend forever!"

Above, we thank the many people who helped us make this book, and list many books and Web sites you may want to explore, on your own or with a parent or teacher.